BOOK OF
Mint

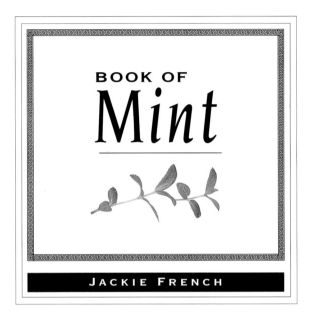

BOOK OF
Mint

JACKIE FRENCH

HarperCollins*Publishers*

First published in 1993
by HarperCollins Publishers
London

First published in Australia in 1993 by
Angus&Robertson, an imprint of HarperCollins Publishers

© Jackie French 1993

*The author asserts the moral right to be identified
as the author of this work.*

*A CIP catalogue record for this book is available
from the British Library*

ISBN 0 00 412897-4

Printed in Hong Kong

CONTENTS

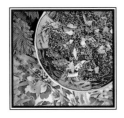

MINT

A BANK OF SWEET HERBS

'Do you mean to say,' said my father, 'that they really eat mint with lamb?'
I said they did, and that it was delicious. He shook his head thoughtfully
'What a funny country,' he said.

~

MYSELF, MY TWO COUNTRIES, X. M. BOLESTIN, 1936

Mint was — and still is — a wild plant, growing rampant by streams
and in wet ditches. Its scent is unmistakable, sweet and cool and
fragrant. It is so familiar in so many modern products — from
toothpaste to cough mixture — that sniffing the real thing may remind
you more of chewing gum than a bank of sweet herbs.

The Romans believed eating mint would increase intelligence. Mint
travelled with the Roman army, both as a kitchen and medicinal herb
(wounds were washed in mint), gradually spreading throughout Europe.
Table-tops rubbed with mint leaves symbolised hospitality.

True Mint Sauce

*Mint sauce is common — good
mint sauce is rare. Take ½ cup
of chopped fresh mint —
different mints will give
different tastes. Add 1 tbspn
of brown sugar; leave for
30 minutes then add 2 cups
(16 fl oz) of white wine
vinegar — the best you can
buy. (Red wine vinegar makes
a different, but equally good,
sauce.) Bring to the boil; take
off the heat at once and let it
stand at least a day,
preferably a month, before you
use it. Mint sauce can be
stored for a year in the
refrigerator. Fresh mint sauce
is harsh; matured mint sauce
makes you realise why it is
eaten with roast lamb.*

By the Middle Ages mint was a common
monastery garden plant, both in the medicinal
and kitchen gardens, and was used to whiten the
teeth, to cure mouth ulcers, to heal the bites of
rabid dogs, to relieve wasp stings, to prevent
milk from curdling, and to repel rats and mice.
Of all of these, mint was probably only effective
in soothing the wasp stings. It was believed that
if you placed mint near an ailing beehive, the
bees would recover.

it [mint] ... stirs up the minds to a greedy taste in meat

~

PLINY, ROMAN NATURALIST.

Orange and Mint Sauce

~ 1 cup chopped mint

~ 1 tbspn brown sugar

~ 1 tbspn redcurrant jelly

*~ grated rind of 2 oranges (no
white pith)*

~ juice of 1 orange

~ 2 tbspns red wine vinegar

~ 2 tbspns water

*Put all the ingredients into a
saucepan and boil for 5
minutes. Bottle and keep in a
cool place or refrigerate once
opened. This sauce becomes
thicker once it cools.*

7
~

Mint Relish for Curry

Pound together till amalgamated, 1 tbspn salt, 2 tbspns mint and the juice of a lime or lemon.

Peach and Raspberry Soup with Mint

4 SMALL SERVES

~ 1 cup raspberries
~ 375 g (13 oz) white peaches, peeled and stoned
~ 2 cups (16 fl oz) water
~ ½ cup (4 oz) sugar
~ 1 cup (8 fl oz) light red wine
~ ½ tspn grated orange zest (no white pith)
~ 1 tspn finely chopped mint
~ Sour (soured) cream

Blend all the ingredients. Serve cold, with a dash of sour cream.

Mint Julep

~ a little crushed ice
~ a sprig of eau de cologne mint
~ 2 tspns of sugar syrup (half water half sugar)
~ a dash of bourbon whisky

Place all the ingredients in a tall glass, stir well, then fill the glass with more crushed ice.

The scent of mint was supposed to stop a person losing their temper, and royal ambassadors carried sprigs in their pockets. Interestingly, recent research at the University of Cincinnati in the United States has indicated that sniffing mint may improve your concentration; and several large Japanese companies pipe minute amounts of mint oil through the air-conditioning systems to invigorate workers and increase productivity. Mint sauce was being made in Britain as early as the third century; by the sixth century it was used as a tooth cleanser. Elizabethan sailors used pennyroyal on long voyages to purify their drinking water (or at least mask its bad taste). All the mints have been used as breath fresheners from the earliest recorded herbal advice.

Mint, or *Mentha*, is named after the nymph Minthes, who was turned into a mint bush by Pluto's jealous wife Proserpine, so that she would forever be trampled under people's feet. I'm not sure why Proserpine made Minthes smell so good — perhaps to keep people treading on her. Though there are hundreds of 'named' mints, there are probably only about 25 distinct species of *Mentha*. Most of these interbreed enthusiastically and their offspring also interbreed, so that there are perhaps 2000 to 3000 hybrids.

The English combine mint with vinegar and eat it with lamb, or add it to fruit salads, or add a touch to boiled new potatoes or boiled carrots or peas with butter; in the Middle East mint is often dried and sprinkled as garnish; in Asia mint is added as a major salad ingredient and in the United States it's imbibed with Kentucky bourbon.

Mint is an incredibly adaptable kitchen herb. It can be added to sweet or savoury dishes. Just the faintest touch of mint will bring out other flavours and when it's used more liberally it has a range of flavours of its own.

Woe unto you, Pharisees! For ye tithe mint and rue and all manner of herbs, and pass over judgement and the love of God.

~

LUKE,1:.42

Peach and Raspberry Soup with Mint

9
~

GROWING MINT – THE HERB FOR 'BLACK FINGERS'

If one wanted to tell completely all the virtues, species and names of mint, one would have to be able to say how many fishes swim in the red sea, or the number of sparks Vulcan can count flying from the vast furnaces of Etna.

~

STRABO, NINTH CENTURY GERMAN ABBOT

All mints are perennial. Most mints (though not all) need a moist position; most need semi-shade to full sun; a few tolerate exposed positions and some tolerate almost total shade. Nearly all mints are incredibly adaptable and if they don't like where you've put them, they will send their runners over to a better spot.

Though most mints produce seed, they often don't breed true to type. Mints are best grown from division, cuttings or runners. Basically, if you get any bit of mint — stem, root or runner — and plant it in water or damp soil, it will probably grow. There is no such thing as 'black fingers' when it comes to mint.

Mint propagation is usually done commercially in autumn, but it is almost impossible to kill mint, which is perhaps one reason why mint has spread so far around the world. Even neglected gardens usually have some mint sprawling in a damp corner by the downpipe — at least they did until the last few decades when cuttings were no longer handed freely over the fence and gardeners stopped relying on their back garden for their herbs and fruit and vegetables. Only a few cooks now make their own mint sauce, preferring the bright green variety bought from supermarkets. Commercial mint sauce tastes of toothpaste and vinegar.

Commercial mint plants can be harvested for 5 or 6 years; in the garden they should last forever.

Pea and Mint Soup

SERVES 4

~ 1 lettuce heart
~ 5 cups fresh peas
~ 1 small shallot (spring onion, scallion)
~ 5 cups (1 ¼ qt) chicken stock
~ 1 cup (8 fl oz) sour (soured) cream
~ 1 dessertspoon finely chopped mint
~ ground black pepper to taste.

Place the lettuce, peas, shallot and stock into a saucepan and simmer until the peas are cooked. Purée the mixture and add the sour cream, mint and black pepper. Serve either chilled or heat gently, so that it doesn't curdle.

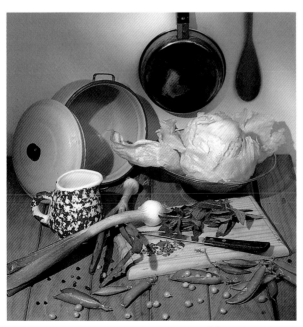

Chilli Prawns with Grapefruit and Mint

ᛘᗯᡗ

4 SMALL SERVES

~ *3 cups cooked prawns (shrimp)*

~ *½ grapefruit, sliced, with pith and membranes removed*

~ *3 cloves garlic, chopped*

~ *1 small red chilli, chopped*

DRESSING

~ *½ cup (4 fl oz) olive oil*

~ *juice of 2 limes*

~ *finely chopped mint*

~ *salt and pepper to taste*

Combine the prawns, grapefruit, garlic and chilli. Toss gently in the dressing made from the remaining ingredients. Serve chilled as a lunch dish, or as an appetiser.

Apple and Mint Salad

ᛘᗯᡗ

4 SMALL SERVES TO ACCOMPANY ANOTHER DISH

~ *2 red apples, chopped (unpeeled)*

~ *1 cucumber, chopped and seeded*

~ *1 red capsicum (sweeet pepper), sliced*

~ *2 thspns chopped mint*

~ *3 thspns olive oil*

~ *1 thspn balsamic vinegar*

Toss all the ingredients together gently. Serve at once.

RUST

Mint is incredibly healthy. The only real problem is rust. Affected plants may have reddish orange 'rust'-like patches on their leaves, or may simply brown and die back.

Rust is more likely to occur where there are great fluctuations in temperature. Often the mint plant will 'outgrow' a mild attack of rust. Cut back the mint if it is badly affected; dip the sound leaves and runners in vinegar and plant them in another area.

Mint can be sprayed with horsetail tea (*Equisetum arvense*) to inhibit rust. Cover 1 cup horsetail with 6 cups (1½ qt) of water. Simmer for 30 minutes and let it stand overnight. Dilute with 3 parts water; strain and use as a spray.

HOW TO CONTROL RAMPANT MINT

The best way to control rampant mint is to mow it regularly. This will eventually kill it. Don't try to pull it out because there'll always be a root that you've missed.

Alternatively, you can grow mint in a pot and plant the pot in the ground, not the mint, so the runners can't escape. Or grow it in a large tub, or thrust slate around the plant to stop the runners spreading.

Mint Lawns

Most mints are prostrate plants but their flower spikes can rise to 1m (39 in), which is too high for a lawn plant. We grow mints under the fruit trees, where they are slashed a couple of times a year and the rest of the time are left to sprawl.

Two mints are suitable for areas around the house and can make a lovely sward. These are creeping pennyroyal (*Mentha pulegium* var. *decumbens*) and Corsican mint (*Mentha requienii*).

Corsican mint is a low-growing mint, suitable only for shady, moist, fertile spots. It won't take a great deal of heavy usage but if your lawn is rarely walked on (and you don't have resident skateboarders) you might consider placing paving stones around the lawn to step on, and forgoing grass in favour of the bright green shiny gloss of Corsican mint.

Creeping pennyroyal is more hardy and will take a reasonable amount of traffic. It needs moisture and fertile soil but will tolerate much more sun than Corsican mint, though it still prefers dappled light.

If you want to give your mint lawn a pick-me-up, scatter over a good top dressing of soil or, even better, good compost, and water well.

Apple and Mint Salad

13
~

Mint Jelly

This can be made with spearmint, or eau de cologne mint. I prefer apple mint or ginger mint. Ginger mint jelly is delicious with baked apples. Apple mint jelly is good with cold roast pork.

~ *1 kg (2 lb) Granny Smith apples*

~ *5 cups (1¼ qt) water*

~ *juice of 3 lemons*

~ *a bunch of mint, finely chopped*

~ *about 500g (1 lb) sugar (more may be needed)*

Don't peel or core the apples. Chop them roughly and boil them with the water and lemon juice until soft. Strain off the juice and only the rind and peel of the apple should be left. Add 500g (1 lb) of sugar for every 2¼ cups (19 fl oz) liquid. Add the mint and stir till the sugar dissolves. Boil until a little of the liquid sets into a blob in cold water. Bottle and seal while hot.

The mint can be strained out after about 10 minutes of cooking, but I prefer it left in, as long as it is finely chopped.

STORING MINT

Mint dries well, though the flavour is changed in the process. Don't use dried mint in fruit salads or with new vegetables, though it is excellent sprinkled onto many Middle Eastern dishes using curd cheese, or yoghurt.

Pick mint to be dried as soon as the dew on it has dried. Hang it in a dark, airy place in small bunches. (If mint is hung in direct sunlight it will lose colour and flavour.)

When the mint leaves are so dry they crumble to dust, strip them from the stalks and pulverise them between your fingers, then store the crumbly powder in an airtight jar till needed. The dried mint should stay pungent for at least a year.

QUICK FREEZING MINT

Pick good sprightly mint; dip it in boiling water for a few seconds then plunge it into cold water. Shake off excess moisture, pack the mint in plastic bags and place in the freezer. Don't put too many in at once — the faster the mint freezes the better. Use immediately after thawing at room temperature.

WHICH MINT TO GROW?

*...the women cultivated a herb corner, stocked with... peppermint,
pennyroyal, horehound, camomile...peppermint tea was made rather as a
luxury than a medicine; it was brought out on special occasions and
drunk from wine glasses; and the women had a private use for the
pennyroyal, though judging from appearances, it was not very effective.*

~

FLORA THOMPSON, *LARK RISE TO CANDLEFORD*, 1939

It is easy to become a mint addict. Mints grow so
easily (all you need is waste ground and a bit of
someone else's mint) and they can look
spectacular with their tall flower spikes in
summer. One of my great pleasures is to take
visitors on a 'smelling' tour of the garden,
sniffing at this leaf and that.

Mint Honey

*Warm the honey slightly.
For every cup (8 fl oz) of
warm honey, add 1 teaspoon
mint leaves. Seal in a jar.
Place the jar in a warm place;
leave it for 3 weeks. Heat
again so it runs freely, and
strain out the mint. Mint
honey will keep for years. If it
candies, heat it again.*

Orange Salad

4 SMALL SERVES

~ *4 oranges chopped, (pith
and membrane removed)*

~ *1 tspn sesame oil*

~ *1 tspn red wine vinegar*

~ *onion, very finely chopped
(until almost transparent)*

~ *very finely chopped mint*

*Toss all the ingredients
together gently.*

Minted Onions

If you don't like the smell of onions, the acrid odour is slightly disguised in this dish.

~ *3 large onions, chopped*

~ *4 thspns white wine vinegar*

~ *1 thspn dried mint*

~ *a touch of salt*

Combine all the ingredients and leave to marinate for at least an hour. Serve as a salad.

Spearmint Sorbet

~ *1 cup (8 fl oz) water*

~ *1 cup (8 oz) sugar*

~ *1 bunch mint*

~ *juice of 1 lemon*

~ *2 egg whites, well beaten*

Boil the water, sugar and mint together for 5 minutes. Strain it, then add the lemon juice and the egg whites. Freeze the mixture stirring it three times during the freezing process. Don't serve the sorbet frozen solid; let it defrost slightly.

While collecting mint is fun, labelling the mints you find may not be so simple. Mint hybridises readily and its hybrids have a tendency to revert to other forms. Even nursery catalogues may name their mints inaccurately, and some mints share their common name with several others. There are at least four 'apple' mints, for example, and at least two 'orange' mints. Where there doesn't seem to be consensus on a plant's derivation, I have simply given the common name, especially in the case of mints like basil mint and ginger mint, that are easily recognised for garden use by their scents.

Spearmint (**Mentha *x* spicata***)*

Spearmint is perhaps the most common culinary mint and until the seventeenth century was the most commonly used medicinal mint. In the sixteenth century it was known as 'spere mynte', reflecting the spear-shaped leaves and spear shape of the plant. It was also formerly known as *Mentha viridis*, a reference to its bright green colour.

Spearmint is native to the Mediterranean region and can still be found wild in damp shady places, usually near habitation. It is a long-leaved mint, bright green, with a strong spearmint flavour — quite different from peppermint — perhaps best described as a 'chewing gum' flavour. It is the least pungent of the common mints and enhances the taste of new peas, new potatoes, carrots and beans.

Spearmint is grown mostly from division, or by planting stem cuttings or roots. Even though the plant may set seed, it rarely breeds true. It prefers moist, fertile, semi-shaded soil but will tolerate direct sunlight and quite dry ground. Where conditions are right it will spread very quickly. Spearmint tea is an old remedy for nausea. It was also prescribed (less successfully) for the hiccups.

Unlike peppermint, spearmint is slightly diuretic. It has been used to treat kidney inflammations.

Curly Mint (Mentha spicata *var.* crispata)

This is a form of spearmint. The leaves are crinkly and bright green. It is a very common mint, and one of the varieties often used for mint sauce.

Spearmint Ointment for Chapped Hands
✺

Cook 2 cups of spearmint in 2 cups (16 fl oz) of oil on very low heat for 30 minutes. Take off the heat, strain out the leaf remnants and add 3 tablespoons of beeswax. Mix well, place in pots and allow to cool. If this is intended to be kept for several months, add the contents of a vitamin E capsule to help preserve it.

Potato, Mint and Onion Raita
✺

SERVES 2–8, DEPENDING ON WHAT OTHER SIDE DISHES ARE SERVED

~ 1 potato, boiled and diced

~ 1 small onion, chopped

~ 2 tbspns mint

~ 1 cup (8 fl oz) natural (plain) yoghurt

~ ½ tspn garam masala

~ chilli powder, to taste

Combine all the ingredients. Cool for an hour. Serve as an accompaniment to curries.

Stewed Dried Beans

SERVES 4

~ 500 g (1 lb) dried haricot
beans

~ 1 onion, chopped

~ ½ cup (4 fl oz) olive oil

~ 4 cups (1 l) hot water

~ 1 garlic clove, chopped

~ 1 sprig mint

~ lemon juice

*Wash the beans — don't soak
them. Sauté the onion in the
heated olive oil, add the beans
and cook slowly till the beans
have absorbed most of the oil.
Add the hot water, garlic and
mint. Don't add salt or the
beans will toughen. Cover the
pan and stew the beans as
slowly as possible until all the
liquid has evaporated.
Serve hot or cold with a
drizzle of lemon juice.*

Camphor Mint Flea
Powder

*Mix 3 parts camphor mint
leaves with 3 parts lavender
flowers and 1 part wormwood
leaves.
Dry the leaves. When very dry
pound to a powder, and ruffle
it through your pet's hair to
deter fleas.*

Horsemint (Mentha alopecurioides)

This is an enormous mint, up to 2 m (6 ft 7 in)
high, with sharply pointed serrated leaves. It is a
well-known wild mint, happy in wet places, and
one of the earliest mints mentioned in herbal
remedies. The flowers are small and purple, on
long narrow spikes.
Horsemint has a powerful smell, not as pleasant
as other mints. In medieval times it was
simmered in vinegar to cure dandruff; the juice
was dropped down earholes 'to cure the worms
that dwells therein'. The warm tea made from
horsemint was guaranteed to cure the skin disease
known as 'king's evil'.

Watermint (Mentha aquatica)

A low-growing mint, only suitable for a moist
spot, often found wild in England. It likes the
banks of ponds and creeks or can be found in
waste wet ground such as ditches. It needs semi-
shade. It is very strong smelling and not as fresh
or pleasant as most other mints. In the Middle
Ages watermint was the main mint used as a
strewing herb to keep away pests and to sweeten
the often rank odour of medieval halls. In Africa
the root bark is used for diarrhoea and colds.
Watermint's appearance can be variable,
sometimes up to 1 m (39 in) tall, but often much
smaller, with lavender to red flowers in late
summer to late autumn. It will set seed but is
best grown by planting a runner or root.

Japanese Mint (**Mentha arvensis**)

Japanese mint is so called because it is widely cultivated in Japan, as well as elsewhere. It is one of the chief commercial sources of menthol, though *Mentha arvensis* oil is inferior in flavour to true peppermint oil.

Cardinal Mint (**Mentha cardinalis**)

This mint has dull green, pointed, slightly furry leaves. The scent is clear and sweet. Cardinal mint is slightly less rampant than many other mints. It forms long stalks some time before flowering, giving it a bushy appearance even though it spreads by runners. Cardinal mint was one of the nosegay mints sniffed to ward off the plague, and one of the ingredients in medieval church incense.

While not suitable for mint sauce, cardinal mint is good in teas and cooking where the true rich mint flavour is not needed.

Cardinal mint prefers semi-shade, good soil and moisture, but is quite adaptable. Propagate by pulling up a runner.

Mentha arvensis

Artichokes, Broad Beans and Mint

SERVES 2

~ 6 artichoke hearts

~ 1 cup broad beans

~ 2 tbspns butter

~ ½ cup (4 fl oz) cream

~ 1 tbspn fresh mint, chopped

~ 2 egg yolks

Steam the artichoke hearts for 15 minutes. Sauté the beans in the heated butter for 5 minutes. Mix in the cream, mint and egg yolks and heat very slowly until thickened. Serve hot.

Tarata

~ ½ cup (4 fl oz) olive oil

~ 3 green peppers (sweet peppers), sliced

~ 1 large eggplant (aubergine), thinly sliced

~ 1 large onion, chopped

~ 1 sprig mint, finely chopped

~ 2 garlic cloves, crushed

~ 3 cups (24 fl oz) natural (plain) yoghurt

Heat the olive oil and sauté the green peppers, eggplant and onion until the onion is very soft. Remove from the heat and allow to cool. Add the mint and garlic and fold in the yoghurt. Serve with curries.

Variegated Ginger Mint (Mentha x gentilis 'variegata')

The 'ginger' of this mint refers to the colour, not the flavour or the scent. It is about 1 m (39 in) high, with a golden variegation, especially on young leaves. It tolerates both moist and dry conditions, and the flowers can be spectacular in long spikes.

English Mint; Horsemint (Mentha longifolia)

A common mint, with long coarse leaves, often used for mint sauce, though spearmint or peppermint is much better — though that is a matter of habit and preference. It is a good salad mint as the perfume doesn't overpower, as peppermint does.

English mint prefers moist, fertile soil and semi-shade. It will survive, but not spread, in full sun and dry conditions. Propagate by seed (though this may not be true to type) or by runners or roots.

Black Peppermint (Mentha x piperata)

Peppermint is a hybrid between spearmint (*Mentha spicata*) and wild water mint (*Mentha aquatica*). Peppermint grows taller than spearmint, up to 100 cm (39 in). Peppermint has a stalked leaf, while spearmint has a sessile, non-stalked leaf. The two main forms are white and black peppermint.

Though it is now one of the most common herbs, peppermint was first recorded in 1696 when the botanist Ray published a brief description of a new 'pepper tasting' mint found by Dr Eales of Hertfordshire in England. In his *Historia Plantarum*, 1704, Ray called the mint 'Peper mint' or '*Mentha palustris*', referring to the places where it prefers to grow. Even though most people don't agree with Ray that the mint tastes of pepper, the name has been retained. It was first prescribed for diarrhoea, and does make the associated stomach cramps less painful.

Tomato and Basil Mint Salad

Sprinkle sliced tomatoes with basil mint; dress with 5 parts olive oil mixed with 1 part lemon juice. Add salt and pepper to taste.

Classic Tabouli

~ 3 cups Egyptian mint, chopped

~ 2 cups (6 oz) cracked wheat or burghul, soaked

~ 1 small onion, finely chopped

~ 2 tomatoes, cut in wedges

~ 6 garlic cloves, chopped

DRESSING:

~ 1 part lemon juice

3 parts olive oil

~ salt and pepper to taste

Combine all the salad ingredients and toss with the lemon juice and olive oil dressing.

Mentha piperata

Pineapple Mint Pork Chops

~ 4 pork chops
~ 3 slices bacon, chopped
~ 2 tbspns olive oil
~ 6 garlic cloves
~ 3 tbspns chopped pineapple mint
~ 1 sage leaf
~ ½ cup (4 fl oz) white wine

Fry the pork chops and bacon in the hot oil until the chops are brown. Add the garlic, pineapple mint and sage, and fry till the chops are cooked. Remove the chops, pour in the white wine and let it bubble until almost evaporated. Pour the sauce over the chops and serve hot.

Peppermint leaves yield from 1 to .8 per cent essential oil, with up to 40 kg (90 lb) of oil harvested per hectare (2 ½ acres). Peppermint oil is pale yellow and is used to flavour chewing gum, toothpaste, sweets, jellies, cigarettes (menthol mild...), liqueurs, medicines, soaps and many others. Peppermint has one of the highest oil content of any of the mints. Both the leaves and the tops of the plant are collected at the beginning of the flowering period. They contain 1—3 per cent of essential oil, of which menthol is the main component.

The scent of peppermint is wonderful and the tea made from it is extremely rich. Peppermint's sharp, penetrating odour has been used to trace leaks in pipes. Peppermint tea is prescribed for gall bladder pains, colic and flatulence — 1 teaspoon to 1 cup (8 fl oz) of water three times a day.

Peppermint is widely used for colds — it induces perspiration, it is a mild antiseptic for sore throats, and helps allay nausea. It is also a mild sedative and helps relieve tension headaches and lessens stomach cramps. It is used in baths and as an infusion to soothe cuts and rashes. (Note: some people are allergic to peppermint oil.)

In days gone by, peppermint branches used to be strewn around barns to keep rats away. This doesn't work — though it may disguise the scent of stored feed slightly.

Peppermint is a vigorous, prostrate plant, with the flower stalks reaching 50 cm (20 in) in fertile, moist soil, though they can be much smaller in dry country. Peppermint flowers appear in midsummer, on long terminal spikes with purple (sometimes white) flowers. Black peppermint tends to be slightly purple around the leaves and stems; white peppermint usually is not.

The richer and moister the soil, the better peppermint will grow, though it doesn't tolerate very wet areas or free-standing water. It grows best in semi-shade but will tolerate full sunlight or full, though not deep, shade. It can also be grown in a pot on the windowsill, as long as the pot is kept wet — try standing it in a saucer of water.

Peppermint rarely sets seed and must be grown by division or cuttings. Either pull up a piece of root and plant it, or take a piece of stem and either plant it in moist soil in semi-shade, or leave it in water till it roots.

White Peppermint (Mentha piperata *var.* officinalis)

This is slightly higher in menthol than black peppermint. The leaves are a clearer green.

Chicken and Cabbage Salad

~ 250 g (8 oz) shredded chicken (preferably boiled, but roasted will do)
~ 1 small onion, finely chopped
~ ¼ of a small cabbage, finely chopped (Chinese cabbage preferably)
~ 2 tbspns shredded rau ram leaves
~ ½ cup (4 fl oz) white vinegar
~ 1 tspn fish sauce
~ a pinch of sugar
~ salt (optional)

Combine the chicken, onion, cabbage and rau ram. Use the remaining ingredients to make a dressing.

Eau de Cologne Mint (Bergamot Mint, Orange Mint, Lavender Mint) — *(*Mentha piperita *var.* citrata*)*

This is the classic mint julep mint and one of the most wonderfully scented. The scent in fact can vary from plant to plant — hence the multiplicity of names — or perhaps the perfume just varies in the mind of those who sniff it. Its former name was *Mentha odorata*.
The leaves of eau de cologne mint are dark green to purple tinged and the mauve flowers grow in dense terminal spikes. It is taller growing than most mints – ours grow to 1 m (39 in) high in semi-shade and about 50 cm (20 in) high in full sunlight. This variety is very tolerant of moisture or dry soils, though with plenty of water it can become rampant. The flowers are pretty, and pale purple; the leaves are greenish purple red and become darker in winter.
Dry your handkerchiefs on a patch of eau de cologne mint; throw a handful of leaves into a hot bath; cover a jar full with brandy or vinegar for a skin tonic and perfume.

Pennyroyal; Pudding Grass; Fleabane (Mentha pulegium)

This is a medieval herb and pest repellent, native to Europe, North Africa and western Asia. The name 'pulegium' was given to pennyroyal by the Romans (probably Pliny) after pulex, the flea — pennyroyal has a long history as an effective flea repellent. (Another name for pennyroyal is fleabane.) Both the fresh plant and the smoke from the burning leaves were used to fumigate flea-ridden rooms.

Mentha piperita var. *citrata*

Pennyroyal was originally considered a thyme and was designated 'the royal thyme', or 'puliol royal' — hence the name pennyroyal. Pennyroyal has tiny grey-green leaves, much softer than most mints. The flowers are pale lavender, appearing in midsummer to early autumn, borne in clusters on the leaf axils. The scent is richer than most mints, a cross between camphor and peppermint. Pennyroyal prefers moist, sandy soils in a sunny or semi-shaded position but tolerates quite dense shade.

At one time pennyroyal was used in cooking, mostly to disguise the scent of offal or elderly meat. Its nickname was 'pudding grass' and it was used in blood puddings too. With the advent of refrigeration, pennyroyal is no longer fashionable as a cooking herb.

Pennyroyal was also used as an abortifacient, though its action was extremely violent and needed large, often fatal, doses to be effective. Experienced midwives selected other herbs and left pennyroyal alone. An excess of pennyroyal can lead to kidney damage and it should be used sparingly.

Creeping Pennyroyal (Mentha pulegium *var.* decumbens)

This is the prostrate pennyroyal, a useful aromatic ground cover. Pennyroyal makes a lovely lawn for a moist part of the garden, especially under trees or shrubs or along a damp path. It is also a good matting plant for deep, dark pathways between raised garden beds, where the clear mint perfume is exuded as one treads on it. Pennyroyal flower spikes stand about 1 m (39 in) high.

Dogs love to roll on pennyroyal lawns. It may help them to get rid of fleas. Bees also love it. The fresh leaves can be rubbed on the skin to ease the itch of insect bites. In the eastern Mediterranean region pennyroyal is used as a dye. The colour it gives depends on the mordant used.

Plant pennyroyal seed in spring when the ground is warm enough to sit on. Each plant should be about 15–20 cm (6–8 in) apart. Keep the young plants well watered in dry weather and protect them from heavy

Three-Melon Antipasto with Forest Mint and Feta

❧

Combine chunks of honeydew melon, watermelon, rockmelon and feta cheese.

For every cup of melon, add a tablespoon of finely chopped forest mint.

Dress with 1 part lemon juice and 1 part olive oil.

Mint Nut Rissoles

❧

~ *1 cup (4 oz) chopped walnuts*

~ *1 cup (4 oz) chopped pecans*

~ *1 cup (4 oz) chopped hazelnuts*

~ *1 cup (4 oz) chopped, shelled sunflower seeds*

~ *1 onion, chopped*

~ *2 cups cooked rice*

~ *1 tspn chopped mint*

~ *1 tspn chopped parsley*

~ *2 eggs*

~ *oil for frying*

Boil the rice; allow to cool. Combine all the ingredients, form into small rissoles, and fry till firm and browned Serve as a main course.

frost — though pennyroyal will tolerate light frost.

Creeping pennyroyal can also be propagated by root division in autumn or spring, or from cuttings taken in summer.

Organy tea

This is a traditional pennyroyal tea taken at the onset of a cold, or to regularise delayed menstruation. Pennyroyal should always be used with extreme caution as it can lead to kidney damage and should *never* be used during pregnancy.

Corsican Mint (Mentha requienii)

A small, low-growing, creeping, bright-leaved mint. The tiny leaves are covered with minute hairs, almost too small to notice. It needs moist ground; a patch of dry weather can soon kill it, especially in summer. It doesn't tolerate heat as well as most of the other mints. The flowers, in groups of about 6, are pale lavender.

Corsican mint is perfect to grow in the cracks of rocks or between cool moist paving stones in semi-shade. It forms a glossy mat, almost like

lawn, with a stunning, clear menthol perfume when it is trodden on —
though it will tolerate only light or occasional traffic.
Corsican mint has a mild mint flavour, and the leaves are much more
tender than the large-leaved mints. It is lovely with boiled new
potatoes, or carrots in butter. I have seen Corsican mint seed advertised
but it is best propagated by dividing a clump.

Apple Mint (Mentha suaveolens)

A soft, round-leaved mint with soft woolly stems and leaves. It grows to
about 90 cm (35 in), and has a strong apple scent as well as strong
undertones of classic mint. The opposite leaves do not have petioles.
Apple mint grows well either in almost total shade or on a sunny bank,
and spreads rapidly. It will also tolerate occasional mowing and forms a
dense carpet under fruit trees, rearing up only when it blooms. The
flowers are white to pink.
Apple mint is a European native, usually found in damp ditches. It is
propagated by division.

*Variegated Apple Mint (*Mentha suaveolens *var.* variegata)

Variegated apple mint is similar to ordinary apple mint, but with
irregular patches of white on the leaves, which are slightly brighter and
paler than the true apple mint. Variegated apple mint is perhaps the
most temperamental of all the common mints and needs cosseting. It
doesn't like frost, or excessive heat, or excessive moisture, or drying out.
It also has a tendency to revert to the green form. Propagate variegated
apple mint by cuttings.

Crystallised Apple Mints

Dip each dry apple mint leaf first into well-beaten egg white, then into caster (superfine) sugar. Dry in an airy place (not the refrigerator). Store in an airtight jar until needed — though they will soften after a few hours.

Serve after dinner and with afternoon tea, and use them to decorate cakes.

Lychees and Champagne with Pineapple Mint

~ 2 cups lychees

~ 1 cup grapefruit segments

~ 1 cup seedless green grapes

~ 2 tbspns chopped pineapple mint.

Combine all the ingredients and top with champagne.

Pineapple Mint
(Mentha suaveolens *var.* variegata)

This, too, is a variegated apple mint, like ordinary apple mint, with round, pale, furry leaves but a quite different scent — like pineapple, though the leaves need to be crushed to release the scent. Some cultivars are not strongly scented — you may have to sniff around. Our pineapple mint appears to have lost much of its characteristic odour with age.

Vietnamese Mint;
Rau Ram (Polygonum mentha)

This is a long-leaved plant with slightly variegated leaves in green and purple with a hint of yellow (this sounds spectacular, but isn't).
Vietnamese mint tolerates light frost but extremely heavy frost will kill it. Our Vietnamese mint dies down each winter but revives in spring when the frosts are over.

Vietnamese mint will take considerable heat and sunshine — I have seen it grown in a hot courtyard — but it also tolerates wet soil and semi- or almost total shade. Propagate Vietnamese mint by picking a stem and standing it in water till it sprouts; or by dividing the clump with a sharp spade; or by pulling up a piece of root and planting it.

Basil Mint

This is a shiny-leaved bushy mint with small leaves, narrowing at the top, and tiny flowers. It smells distinctly of basil. Unlike common basil, it is a perennial and frost resistant, so is available all year. Unlike basil, basil mint is best eaten raw as the flavour changes slightly when cooked. When using basil mint in cooking add the chopped leaves at the end of the cooking time rather than during cooking.

Basil mint is also a fly repellent — though you need a very large bush to make much of a difference in the fly season. A long planter box of basil mint along the windowsill does help prevent flies from coming indoors, though if you're cooking steak nothing will keep them away. Basil mint can also be made into a tea to keep flies away from a sheep's dags, or animal wounds.

Pineapple Mint Beer

~ 6 lemons, sliced

~ grated rind of 3 oranges

~ 1 thspn freshly grated
ginger

~ 1 bunch pineapple mint

~ 1 tspn cream of tartar

~ 500 g (1 lb) sugar

~ 1 tspn dried yeast

*Pour 14 cups (3½ qt) boiling
water onto the lemons, grated
orange rind, ginger and
pineapple mint. Add the cream
of tartar and sugar. Allow to
cool until tepid then add the
dried yeast. Leave for 48
hours, strain and bottle. The
beer will be ready in 2 or 3
days.*

*Use corks, not screw tops, for
this beer to prevent the bottles
exploding. Release the pressure
every day if you are keeping it
more than a week.*

Camphor Mint

This is a roundish-leaved, shiny mint, very
strongly camphor scented. It is prostrate and
prefers semi-shade and very moist ground but
survives frost and heat once established. It can
become rampant. The flowers are pale blue, and
very pretty in late summer, on tall flower heads.
Camphor mint has a high oil content and can
sometimes leave an oily residue on the fingers
after touching it.
Don't use camphor mint in cooking. The food
will taste disgusting. It is, however, a very
effective moth repellent. Tie it in bunches and
hang them in cupboards, or slip them in bags
with woollen clothes.

Egyptian Mint

This is one of the largest-leaved mints, relatively
tender and much milder in flavour than most
mints. The leaves are bright green and slightly
crinkled. The flower spikes form long before the
flowers appear, so Eygptian mint looks rather like
a shaggy bush, up to 1 m (39 in) tall. The flowers
are small, pale blue, and grow along the flower
spike in midsummer. They can look very pretty.
Egyptian mint tolerates extreme heat and
dryness, though it grows much faster with
moisture and good soil. It is a very fast growing
mint if the conditions are right.

Eygptian mint is one of the classic ingredients of tabouli, often replaced by the much less piquant parsley, which gives a different effect altogether.

Ginger mint (*not* **Mentha x gentilis**)

This is a long-leaved mint, adaptable to both sun, shade, dry and moist soils, though it grows best in moist semi-shade. It is slightly damaged by heavy frost, but should survive and flourish again the next year.

Fried Zucchini (Courgettes) with Rau Ram

~ 3 tbspns of oil

~ 2 cups zucchini, sliced

~ 1 onion, cut into small wedges

~ 2 garlic cloves, chopped

~ a handful rau ram leaves, chopped

~ 3 tspns fish sauce

Heat the oil and fry the zucchini, onion and garlic on a high heat until the onion turns transparent. Add the rau ram leaves and fish sauce. Simmer 1 minute. Remove the pan from the heat. Serve hot.

Prawn (Shrimp) and Pork Salad

❧

~ *cooked pork belly, thinly sliced*

~ *3 cups cooked prawns (shrimp)*

~ *1 cucumber, peeled, seeded and sliced diagonally*

~ *1 carrot, peeled and sliced diagonally*

~ *3 sticks celery, finely sliced diagonally*

~ *half a cup shredded rau ram leaves*

DRESSING:

~ *1 tbspn fish sauce*

~ *1 garlic clove, crushed*

~ *2 tbspns rice wine vinegar (or dry sherry)*

~ *1 tspn sugar*

TOPPING:

~ *chopped peanuts, chopped chillies and extra rau ram leaves.*

Arrange on a plate the pork, prawns, cucumber, carrot, celery and rau ram leaves. Mix the fish sauce with the garlic, rice wine vinegar and sugar and pour it over the meat and vegetables. Sprinkle generously with the peanuts, chillies and extra rau ram leaves.

NATIVE AUSTRALIAN MINTS

There are six native Australian mints that have the familiar mint fragrance. Four of these are:

River Mint
(Mentha australis)

This is the most common native Australian mint. It grows in wet places, especially in the inland areas. It has bright green opposite leaves and small four-petalled flowers in the leaf axils.

River mint has a strong peppermint scent and taste. It was used by Aboriginal people as a tea for coughs and colds, heated with hot stones, and as an inhalant (the mint was thrown onto hot coals in the fire). It was also used as an abortifacient. Colonial settlers also used river mint in most of the ways they had used peppermint or spearmint in their countries of origin.

River mint is most easily propagated by pulling up a root and transplanting it. It needs plenty of moisture but will tolerate sun or semi-shade.

Slender Mint
(Mentha diemenica)

Another native Australian pennyroyal. It is found in New South Wales, Victoria, Tasmania and South Australia. The leaves are longer than *Mentha satureioides*, but otherwise the two plants are very similar.

Forest Mint
(Mentha laxiflora)

A small mint, to 40 cm (16 in), with incredibly sweet-scented leaves and purple flowers. It likes shady, moist areas and is an excellent, neat addition to the garden.

River Mint Fish

Pull up a few handfuls of river mint. Wet it well and wrap it round a scaled and gutted fish. Place the fish near a hot fire and let it steam in the mint.

Mentha pulegium

Chicken and Barley Soup with Yoghurt

SERVES 4

~ *1 onion, chopped*

~ *60 g (2 oz) butter*

~ *4 cups (1 qt) chicken stock*

~ *1 tbspn pearl barley*

~ *2 tbspns chopped parsley*

~ *600 ml (18 fl oz) natural (plain) yoghurt*

~ *2 tbspns chopped mint*

Sauté the onion in the butter until the onion is transparent. Add the stock, barley and parsley. Simmer until the barley is soft, adding more water if necessary. Add the yoghurt and mint and heat gently so that the soup doesn't curdle. Serve hot.

Native Pennyroyal, Creeping Mint (Mentha satureioides)

Another native Australian mint, found in all mainland states, with small leaves and clusters of tiny white flowers in the leaf axils. It has very strong perfume, especially when trodden on. It isn't quite as sweet as European pennyroyal, though in wild species the scent and flavour can vary considerably.

Native pennyroyal contains pulegone, as do the European and American pennyroyals, and colonial settlers used native pennyroyal in the ways they used to at home, as flea or bedbug repellents, as a mattress filling, or strewn on floors. They, too, tried native pennyroyal as an abortifacient, though any apparent success was probably caused by pennyroyal inducing delayed menstruation, rather than an abortion. As with American and European pennyroyals, any dose high enough to be effective would be toxic.

Native pennyroyal will grow in quite dry areas, including forest floors. It will grow from cuttings, or division or transplanted root, as well as from seed. This is best collected by hanging an old stocking over the seed heads after flowering.

COMPANION PLANTING AND MINT

Pennyroyal and spearmint are said to keep ants away; they don't. Any aromatic substance (even squashed ants) will deter ants, so will the moist soil that pennyroyal prefers. Growing spearmint under roses is said to keep aphid-carrying ants away. My own trials of this have been inconclusive so far, but the roses with spearmint growing round them were more prone to black spot. The aphids did less damage than the black spot.

Sekanjabin

An ancient Persian Mint and Cucumber Drink

~ *4 cups (1 qt) water*
~ *3 cups (1 lb 5 oz) sugar*
~ *2 cups (16 fl oz) good white wine vinegar*
~ *2 tbspns chopped mint*
~ *2 tbspns peeled, finely chopped cucumber*

Boil the water and sugar until the sugar dissolves. Add the remaining ingredients and dilute with iced water. Drink very cold for a wonderfully refreshing drink.

Ayran

A Lebanese Yoghurt Drink

~ *2 cups (16 fl oz) natural (plain) yoghurt*
~ *4 cups (1 qt) cold water*
~ *3 tbspns very finely chopped mint*
~ *a pinch of salt*

Beat all the ingredients together. Serve over crushed ice.

Chocolate Mint Ice Cream

Serves 4–6 or 2 greedy people

~ *1 cup mint leaves*

~ *4 cups (1 qt) cream*

~ *1 cup (7 oz) sugar*

~ *2 egg yolks*

~ *200 g (7 oz) bitter chocolate, grated (if it is sweet use less sugar)*

~ *1 tspn vanilla essence*

Soak the mint leaves in 3 cups (24 fl oz) of cream overnight. Strain.

Heat 1 cup (8 fl oz) of cream with the sugar till the sugar dissolves. Allow to cool. Add the egg yolks and other ingredients. Freeze in an ice cream churn, or in trays, stirring every 20 minutes until frozen.

This is wonderful!

Mint is said to repel cabbage white butterfly. It doesn't do that very effectively either, unless the small seedlings are planted in the middle of a patch of mint. Larger seedlings, with the mint a long way below the affected leaves, can still be devastated.

Spearmint is said to keep bean fly away if it is grown between the rows of beans. I haven't tested this.

Camomile or nettles grown with mint are said to increase its essential oil.

Mint is said to be an excellent companion crop with tomatoes. In my own experiments I have not noticed any difference between the adult tomatoes grown with or without mint, but the tomato seedlings grew faster and more vigorously with mint as a neighbour. However, one season's observation isn't enough to form an opinion.

Mints are wonderful under fruit trees. The mint loves the dappled light and moist, leaf-rich soil, and the trees do better without grass above their roots (grass inhibits the development of small feeder roots). The mint flowers attract pest-controlling predators.

Mints under fruit trees can be mown a couple of times a year and still survive. Geese will eat the grass under the trees and leave the mint. Mint is one of the few ground covers that thrive under English walnut trees.

Mint Sorbet

~ 1 cup (8 fl oz) water

~ 2 tbspns caster (superfine) sugar

~ 2 tbspns chopped mint (peppermint, spearmint, ginger mint are all good)

~ juice of 1 lemon

~ 2 egg whites, whipped

Boil the water and sugar for 5 minutes. Allow to cool. Add the freshly chopped mint. Leave overnight. Strain out the mint. Fold in the lemon juice and egg whites as gently as you can. Freeze. Stir just as the sorbet is beginning to set.

Serve the sorbet slightly soft and grainy. If necessary, take the sorbet out of the freezer 5 minutes before serving.

An alternative is to leave the mint in the sorbet. This makes a greener mix, but is slightly gritty unless the mint is very finely chopped indeed, or puréed in the blender.

Mint sorbet is an excellent after-dinner digestive — a good way to end a rich meal.

If you are keeping mint sorbet for more than a week, make sure it is in a covered, airtight container.

Mint Tea for Colds

~ 1 part yarrow flowers

~ 1 part elder flowers

~ 1 part peppermint leaves

~ 1 part lavender flowers

Dry the flowers on newspaper in a warm, airy place out of direct sunlight.

To make the tea, cover a teaspoon of the mixture with boiling water; strain, and drink hot.

Jars of 'cold tea' look very pretty, with the dark green dried mint leaves and dried flowers.

Mint Tea for Nausea

~ 1 part camomile flowers

~ 12 parts peppermint

~ 2 parts spearmint

~ 1 part lemon balm

~ 1 part fennel seed

Infuse all the ingredients in hot water. Strain the tea and sip slowly as required. Note: this should **not** be taken regularly during pregnancy.

MEDICINAL MINT AND MINT COSMETICS

The ancients entwined their wine cups with pennyroyal, and made crowns of it, which were placed on their heads during their repasts, by the aid of which they hoped to escape the troublesome consequences of too copious libations. On leaving the table, a small quantity of this plant was taken, to facilitate digestion...

~

ALEXIS SOYER, *THE PANTROPHEON*, 1853

Mint was probably one of the earliest herbal remedies discovered. In fact mint must have been hard to miss — the fresh scent of mint when it's trodden on seems to help clear a stuffy head, while the cool scent would lend itself to rubbing on grazes or insect bites. The soothing and cooling effects of mint would have been immediately apparent.

Mint has been found in Egyptian tombs dating back to 1000 BC and it has been part of the Chinese pharmacopoeia for even longer. The Emperor Charlemagne especially ordered it grown for its digestive properties. Mint tea is a classic Arab drink.

It is the numerous oil glands in the leaves that make mint so aromatic. The menthol in peppermint and eau de cologne mint triggers the nerve endings in the skin that respond to cold, and gives an illusion of coolness. Mint oil is also mildly anaesthetic. Mint will soothe itching skin, while the menthol numbs the skin.
Mint oils have medicinal properties; they alleviate flatulence and aid the digestion (yes, after-dinner mints are *GOOD* for you!).
Mint tea is used to help relieve the symptoms of a cold, it soothes a sore throat and acts as an expectorant. It is also used in a large number of cultures as a digestive.

Eau de Cologne Mint Face Wash (for oily skin)

Simmer ½ cup eau de cologne mint in 3 cups (24 fl oz) of water, and ½ cup (4 fl oz) of cider vinegar for 10 minutes. Leave until cool then strain it. Store in the refrigerator.

Mint Lotion for Cracked Hands

Combine 1 tspn apricot oil, 1 tspn olive oil, 1 tspn almond oil and 6 drops of peppermint oil. (Or simmer 1 tbspn of mint in ½ cup (4 fl oz) of water till reduced by three-quarters and add that instead.) If you use the latter, shake the mixture well before using.

Home-made Toothpaste

Moisten and mix orris root (the ground root of the florentine iris) with 1 part peppermint oil to 3 parts safflower or any other bland oil. Mix; store in an airtight jar.

Oatmeal and Peppermint Scrub

Moisten 1 cup (3 oz) of rolled oats with 1 tspn peppermint oil. Mix very well. Use a spoonful of the mixture to wash your hands, rubbing them gently with the perfumed oats. They will be softer, cleaner and fresher than if you had used soap.

Compote of Dried Fruit

SERVES 4

~ 1 cup (4 oz) dried apricots

~ 1 cup (6 oz) dried prunes

~ ½ cup (1 oz) dried pears

~ ½ cup (1 oz) dried apples

~ 2 cups (16 fl oz) water

~ ½ bottle dry cider

~ juice of 2 lemons

~ 1 tbspn finely chopped mint

cream, cinnamon and sugar,

for serving

Combine all the compote ingredients and poach the fruit gently for 5 minutes. Leave them to swell in the liquid. Serve cold with thick (heavy) cream, whipped with a little cinnamon and sugar.

MINT AS AN APHRODISIAC

According to the herbalist Culpeper (1616–54), spearmint 'stirs up venery or bodily lust'.

Culpeper also claimed mint was good for the bites of rabid dogs, and for scabs and blotches in children; it was also a specific for gonorrhoea.

Interestingly, mint has retained its aphrodisiac reputation for animal use, and some stud masters still feed mint to horses and bulls before joining. An ancient Persian custom was for women to eat bread, cheese and mint (with other herbs) at the end of the meal, to keep their husbands faithful.

Hungarian Water

According to a wandering hermit who gave this recipe to Queen Elizabeth of Hungary, the potion is supposed to keep you looking young for decades.
It apparently worked for her, but hasn't been quite so successful since.
Combine 1 tbspn mint leaves, 1 tbspn rosemary leaves, 2 tbspns rose water, the grated peel of 1 orange and 1 lemon and ½ cup (4 fl oz) brandy.
Store in a dark place for a week then strain into dark bottles with tight-fitting lids. Dab on as needed.

MINT AND ANIMALS

Mints put into milk, it neyther sufferth the same to curde, nor to be come thick, insomuch that it layed in curded milke, this would bring the same thinne againe.

~

THE GOOD HOUSEWIFE'S HANDMAID, 1588

According to folklore, mint is a powerful aphrodisiac for stallions and bulls. Stud animals would be given chopped mint in their feed before joining.

Mint is used in some Middle Eastern countries to help animals' milk supply dry up in the latter months of pregnancy. Mint was also added to new milk in thundery weather to stop it turning (I don't know if this works or not).

In Europe mint was strewn over stable floors in winter to reduce the strong smell of ammonia after animals had been kept indoors for months, and to repel fleas.

Peppermint Lip Salve

This will both soothe and protect cracked lips.

Melt 1 tspn beeswax with 10 tspns cocoa butter. Remove from the heat and add 6 drops of peppermint oil. Place the mixture in an old lipstick container, and allow to set.

Moroccan Mint Tea

Heat a large jug (preferably silver). Place into it 1 tbspn green tea (unfermented tea), a handful of fresh mint leaves and lump (cubed) sugar to taste (I like very little, but this traditionally is served quite sweet).

Pour into the jug 4 cups (1 l) of boiling water. Infuse for 5 minutes. Skim off any mint or tea leaves that float to the top. Raise the jug as high as you can, and pour the tea into glasses — this 'aeration' is said to make the tea taste better.

After Dinner Tea

Mint tea can of course be made simply with mint — just pour a cup of boiling water over a teaspoon or two of fresh mint. Different sorts of mint give different flavours. I prefer spearmint, or ginger mint tea. After-dinner tea is far more like conventional tea, flavoured with mint. It helps the digestion; it relaxes; and it also tastes lovely.

Combine 1 part mint leaves with 1 part lemon verbena leaves, 4 parts strawberry leaves and a handful of rose petals.

Dry all the ingredients. Keep in a jar till needed. Brew as you would ordinary tea.

Mint has also been used as an udder salve to treat mastitis in cows and goats — the mint leaves are simmered in oil till the oil turns yellow-green, then rubbed gently into the udder before milking.

Pennyroyal used to be given to cows after they had calved. (One handful of the herb in 4 cups (1 qt) of water, simmered for 5 minutes.) It was supposed to soothe and warm the cow. Given the medicinal properties of pennyroyal this may well have a sound basis — though I wouldn't experiment without veterinary advice.

MINT AND RODENTS

Rats and mice are said to be repelled by the scent of mint, and mint-soaked rags were plugged into rat-holes to send the rodents out the other end. Whether this worked or not may have had little to do with the scent of mint. I've thrust mint-soaked hankies at various white rats and pet mice, and they've sniffed it and gone on eating. But any strong new odour will scare wild rats and mice and send them scuttling in the opposite direction — out through the other end of the hole where the ratters are waiting.

Mint bushes by the doorway and drainpipe are supposed to stop mice and rats entering the house. They don't.

Herbal Digestive Liquor

Don't use dried herbs for this — it will taste like compost. It shouldn't. It is a very good, relaxing, after-dinner drink.

~ 1 tbspn fresh camomile flowers

~ 1 tbspn chopped mint

~ 1 tbspn chopped lemon verbena

~ 1 tbspn chopped lemon or lime balm

~ 2 cloves

~ a sprinkle of cinnamon

~ 1 tspn chopped fresh coriander

~ 1 tbspn chopped lavender flowers

~ 1 dessertspoon sugar

~ rind of 2 lemons (no pith at all)

~ 1 small bottle brandy

Combine all the ingredients in a jar and leave for 8 weeks, shaking the jar every day. Strain out the liquid. Leave for at least a month, preferably a year. Drink in small glasses.

This is also very good during the day — 1 tbspn poured over a glass of cracked ice.

Mint-based Insect Repellent

Mix 1 part pennyroyal oil with 1 part lavender oil, 1 part cider vinegar, 1 part mentholated spirits and 1 part baby oil. Smooth on as needed.

Mint Potpourri

Combine 1 part lemon peel, 1 part orange peel, 2 parts lavender flowers, 1 part bay leaves, 10 parts mint leaves (use a variety of mints if you can), 1 part orris root and 1 part salt.

This potpourri is sweet and fresh. Leave it in open bowls and it will remove musty odours from the room.

GIFTS FROM MINT

The smell rejoiceth the heart of man, for which cause they strew it in chambers and places of recreation, pleasure and repose, and where feasts and banquets are made.

~

GERARD, *HERBAL* (1545–1612)

MINT POSIES

Make posies from a variety of mints — apple mint, eau de cologne mint etc., and give them to your hostess instead of flowers. She can keep them in a vase, use them for cooking — or throw them in a hot bath then climb in too, and enjoy.

SWEET MASSAGE OIL

Fill a small jar with your favourite mints; add a tablespoon or so of brandy. The next day fill the crevices in the mint-filled jar with massage oil. Place the jar on a sunny windowsill and shake the jar every day for 3 weeks. Strain. The oil will be pale yellow. Use for aching muscles, on grazes, or just for pleasure.

TO SWEETEN A ROOM

~ Make a weak tea with half tea and half mint. Let it cool. Spray it around the room.
~ Throw dried mint leaves on an open fire to fill the room with perfume.
~ Place half-dried mint leaves and half-dried mandarin peel in a small box. Throw a pinch on the fire as it dies down. The room will smell sweet in the morning and there will be no smell of old, cold soot in the afternoon.

Mint Foot Powder

Combine 1 cup talcum powder with ½ cup cornflour (cornstarch), 1 tspn peppermint oil and 1 tspn vinegar.

Keep in a sealed jar and use as a dusting powder for the feet.

Mint Bubble Bath

Children love to use this. They'll dive into scented bubbles even when normally they refuse to wash their hair.

Simmer for 20 minutes 1 cup mint (eau de cologne mint, pineapple mint, spearmint — or a combination of several mints), and 2 cups (16 fl oz) water. Cool and strain the liquid. Add half a bottle of shampoo. Put it in a bottle and seal it.

AND FINALLY: THE PERFECT
AFTER-DINNER MINT

It is perhaps admitting a certain bias to say that the after-dinner mint is
the greatest achievement since humans first starting experimenting
with mint. Chocolate is addictive. Adding mint makes it even more
addictive. This recipe is for those who share my prejudice.

Chocolate Mint Leaves

Melt a little good quality cooking chocolate. Add one drop of peppermint oil per tablespoon of chocolate. If the
chocolate seems a little dry, add a little oil or Copha — not water, which will turn it grainy.
Take perfect-looking mint leaves and coat the fronts with the melted chocolate. When they are dry, peel off the leaves
gently. The chocolate will be leaf shaped and delicious. Eat them after dinner or use to decorate cakes — or scoff the
lot before anyone else finds them.

Chocolate Mint Truffles

~ *2 cups (16 fl oz) cream*
~ *half a cup mint leaves or a few drops peppermint oil*
~ *500 g (1 lb) cooking chocolate*
~ *5 tbspns unsalted butter*
~ *cocoa powder or extra chocolate*

Put the cream, mint leaves and butter in a pan and heat gradually till it just starts to simmer. Remove from the heat, strain off the mint, add the chocolate and stir well. Place in the refrigerator to thicken, stirring it every 30 minutes (at least 4 times). Scoop out spoonfuls of the mixture, roll them into a ball, and roll in cocoa or dip in extra melted chocolate. Cool again.

Peppermints

Stir as much icing sugar as you can into a beaten egg white. Add 3 drops of peppermint for every egg white. Shape into small balls and leave to dry. Eat plain, or coat with melted chocolate.

ACKNOWLEDGMENTS

The publisher would like to thank the following organisations in New South Wales, Australia, for supplying various photographic props:

Common Scents Cottage, Dural

Grosvenor Antique Centre, Lindfield

Home & Garden on the Mall, Sky Gardens, Sydney

Herbal Teas by Penelope Sach, Woollahra

~ ~ ~

PHOTOGRAPHY
Scott Cameron Photography Pty Ltd

FOOD STYLING
Lisa Hilton

ILLUSTRATION
Dianne Bradley

COVER PHOTOGRAPHY
Ivy Hansen